MAD LIBS®

COOL M...

By Roger Price and Leonard Stern

PSS!
PRICE STERN SLOAN

PRICE STERN SLOAN
Published by the Penguin Group
Penguin Group (USA) Inc., 375 Hudson Street, New York, New York 10014, USA
Penguin Group (Canada), 90 Eglinton Avenue East, Suite 700,
Toronto, Ontario M4P 2Y3, Canada
(a division of Pearson Penguin Canada Inc.)
Penguin Books Ltd., 80 Strand, London WC2R 0RL, England
Penguin Group Ireland, 25 St. Stephen's Green, Dublin 2, Ireland
(a division of Penguin Books Ltd.)
Penguin Group (Australia), 250 Camberwell Road, Camberwell, Victoria 3124, Australia
(a division of Pearson Australia Group Pty. Ltd.)
Penguin Books India Pvt. Ltd., 11 Community Centre,
Panchsheel Park, New Delhi—110 017, India
Penguin Group (NZ), 67 Apollo Drive, Rosedale, North Shore 0632, New Zealand
(a division of Pearson New Zealand Ltd.)
Penguin Books (South Africa) (Pty.) Ltd., 24 Sturdee Avenue,
Rosebank, Johannesburg 2196, South Africa

Penguin Books Ltd., Registered Offices: 80 Strand, London WC2R 0RL, England

Copyright © 2001 by Price Stern Sloan.
All rights reserved.

Published by Price Stern Sloan,
a division of Penguin Young Readers Group,
345 Hudson Street, New York, New York 10014.

Printed in the United States of America. Published simultaneously in Canada.
No part of this publication may be reproduced, stored in any retrieval system, or transmitted,
in any form or by any means, electronic, mechanical, photocopying, or otherwise,
without the prior written permission of the publisher.

ISBN 978-0-8431-7660-5

33 35 37 39 40 38 36 34

PSS! and MAD LIBS are registered trademarks of Penguin Group (USA) Inc.

MAD LIBS®
INSTRUCTIONS

MAD LIBS® is a game for people who don't like games!
It can be played by one, two, three, four, or forty.

• RIDICULOUSLY SIMPLE DIRECTIONS

In this tablet you will find stories containing blank spaces where words are
left out. One player, the READER, selects one of these stories. The READER
does not tell anyone what the story is about. Instead, he/she asks the other
players, the WRITERS, to give him/her words. These words are used to fill
in the blank spaces in the story.

• TO PLAY

The READER asks each WRITER in turn to call out a word—an adjective or
a noun or whatever the space calls for—and uses them to fill in the blank
spaces in the story. The result is a MAD LIBS® game.

When the READER then reads the completed MAD LIBS® game to the other
players, they will discover that they have written a story that is fantastic,
screamingly funny, shocking, silly, crazy, or just plain dumb—depending
upon which words each WRITER called out.

• EXAMPLE (*Before* and *After*)

"_____!" he said _____
        EXCLAMATION   ADVERB

as he jumped into his convertible _____ and
                                              NOUN

drove off with his _____ wife.
                          ADJECTIVE

"_____*Ouch!*_____!" he said _____*stupidly*_____
        EXCLAMATION   ADVERB

as he jumped into his convertible _____*cat*_____ and
                                              NOUN

drove off with his _____*brave*_____ wife.
                          ADJECTIVE

In case you have forgotten what adjectives, adverbs, nouns, and verbs are, here is a quick review:

An ADJECTIVE describes something or somebody. *Lumpy, soft, ugly, messy,* and *short* are adjectives.

An ADVERB tells how something is done. It modifies a verb and usually ends in "ly." *Modestly, stupidly, greedily,* and *carefully* are adverbs.

A NOUN is the name of a person, place or thing. *Sidewalk, umbrella, bridle, bathtub,* and *nose* are nouns.

A VERB is an action word. *Run, pitch, jump,* and *swim* are verbs. Put the verbs in past tense if the directions say PAST TENSE. *Ran, pitched, jumped,* and *swam* are verbs in the past tense.

When we ask for a PLACE, we mean any sort of place: a country or city *(Spain, Cleveland)* or a room *(bathroom, kitchen.)*

An EXCLAMATION or SILLY WORD is any sort of funny sound, gasp, grunt, or outcry, like *Wow!, Ouch!, Whomp!, Ick!,* and *Gadzooks!*

When we ask for specific words, like a NUMBER, a COLOR, an ANIMAL, or a PART OF THE BODY, we mean a word that is one of those things, like *seven, blue, horse,* or *head.*

When we ask for a PLURAL, it means more than one. For example, *cat* pluralized is *cats.*

MAD LIBS® is fun to play with friends, but you can also play it by yourself! To begin with, DO NOT look at the story on the page below. Fill in the blanks on this page with the words called for. Then, using the words you have selected, fill in the blank spaces in the story.

Now you've created your own hilarious MAD LIBS® game!

HOW TO DATE THE COOLEST GUY/GIRL IN SCHOOL

PLURAL NOUN _____

ADVERB _____

VERB _____

ARTICLE OF CLOTHING _____

BODY PART _____

ADJECTIVE _____

NOUN _____

PLURAL NOUN _____

ANOTHER BODY PART _____

PLURAL NOUN _____

ANOTHER BODY PART _____

NOUN _____

NOUN _____

VERB ENDING IN "ING" _____

ADJECTIVE _____

ADJECTIVE _____

VERB _____

MAD LIBS®
HOW TO DATE THE COOLEST GUY/GIRL IN SCHOOL

It's simple. Turn the _____. Make him/her want

PLURAL NOUN

_____ to date you. Make sure you're always dressed

ADVERB

to _____. Each and every day, wear a/an _____

VERB   ARTICLE OF CLOTHING

that you know shows off your _____ to _____

BODY PART   ADJECTIVE

advantage and make your _____ look like a million

NOUN

_____. Even if the two of you make meaningful

PLURAL NOUN

_____ contact, don't admit it. No hugs or

ANOTHER BODY PART

_____. Just shake his/her _____

PLURAL NOUN   ANOTHER BODY PART

firmly. And remember, when he/she asks you out, even though a

chill may run down your _____ and you can't stop your

NOUN

_____ from _____, just play it _____.

NOUN   VERB ENDING IN "ING"   ADJECTIVE

Take a long pause before answering in a very _____ voice.

ADJECTIVE

"I'll have to _____ it over."

VERB

From COOL MAD LIBS® • Copyright © 2001 by Price Stern Sloan,
a division of Penguin Putnam Books for Young Readers, New York.

MAD LIBS® is fun to play with friends, but you can also play it by yourself! To begin with, DO NOT look at the story on the page below. Fill in the blanks on this page with the words called for. Then, using the words you have selected, fill in the blank spaces in the story.

Now you've created your own hilarious MAD LIBS® game!

CELL PHONES

NOUN _____

BODY PART _____

PLURAL NOUN _____

NOUN _____

PLURAL NOUN _____

PLURAL NOUN _____

PLURAL NOUN _____

PLURAL NOUN _____

VERB ENDING IN "ING" _____

ADVERB _____

BODY PART _____

VERB _____

ADJECTIVE _____

NOUN _____

PLURAL NOUN _____

NOUN _____

NOUN _____

MAD LIBS®
CELL PHONES

No matter where you are these days, you're bound to run into

someone with a cellular _____ attached to his/her _____.
                              NOUN   BODY PART

Even young _____ have _____ phones.
                 PLURAL NOUN   NOUN

Unfortunately, they seem to bring out the worst _____
                                                        PLURAL NOUN

in people. Most cell-phone users talk with raised _____
                                                        PLURAL NOUN

in restaurants, museums, _____, and even in women's
                              PLURAL NOUN

and men's _____. Cell-phone users think nothing of
                PLURAL NOUN

talking at the same time they are _____ their cars. This
                                    VERB ENDING IN "ING"

can be _____ dangerous, especially when they take their
           ADVERB

_____ off the road as they _____. Pedestrian
   BODY PART   VERB

phoners are also a/an _____ hazard. Preoccupied with
                           ADJECTIVE

their conversations, they can easily ignore a red _____ and
                                                        NOUN

step in front of oncoming _____, causing all kinds of
                              PLURAL NOUN

_____ accidents and _____ pile-ups.
   NOUN   NOUN

From COOL MAD LIBS® • Copyright © 2001 by Price Stern Sloan,
a division of Penguin Putnam Books for Young Readers, New York.

MAD LIBS® is fun to play with friends, but you can also play it by yourself! To begin with, DO NOT look at the story on the page below. Fill in the blanks on this page with the words called for. Then, using the words you have selected, fill in the blank spaces in the story.

Now you've created your own hilarious MAD LIBS® game!

SPECIALTY OF THE HOUSE

NAME OF PERSON IN ROOM _____

VERB ENDING IN "ING" _____

BODY PART _____

ANIMAL _____

SAME BODY PART _____

NUMBER _____

PLURAL NOUN _____

NOUN _____

VERB (PAST TENSE) _____

FOOD _____

LIQUID _____

ADJECTIVE _____

COLOR _____

NOUN _____

PLURAL NOUN _____

NUMBER _____

COLOR _____

PLURAL NOUN _____

NOUN _____

MAD LIBS®
SPECIALTY OF THE HOUSE

Here is chef _____'s award- _____
        NAME OF PERSON IN ROOM   VERB ENDING IN "ING"

recipe for roast _____ of _____ : Choose a
                     BODY PART   ANIMAL

_____ weighing about _____ _____ .
   SAME BODY PART   NUMBER   PLURAL NOUN

Remove excess _____ . Add 5 cloves of garlic, peeled and
                    NOUN

_____ . Season with 2 tablespoons of chopped _____ .
VERB (PAST TENSE)   FOOD

Add a tablespoon of _____ . Sprinkle with a touch of
                          LIQUID

_____ salt. Add a pinch of ground _____ _____ .
 ADJECTIVE   COLOR   NOUN

Cook at 350 _____ for _____ minutes. Remove from
              PLURAL NOUN   NUMBER

the oven when the skin is _____ . Serve with mashed
                                 COLOR

_____ and a/an _____ .
 PLURAL NOUN   NOUN

From COOL MAD LIBS® • Copyright © 2001, 1985 by Price Stern Sloan,
a division of Penguin Putnam Books for Young Readers, New York.

MAD LIBS® is fun to play with friends, but you can also play it by yourself! To begin with, DO NOT look at the story on the page below. Fill in the blanks on this page with the words called for. Then, using the words you have selected, fill in the blank spaces in the story.

Now you've created your own hilarious MAD LIBS® game!

MUSIC

NOUN _____

NOUN _____

ADJECTIVE _____

ADJECTIVE _____

BODY PART (PLURAL) _____

BODY PART (PLURAL) _____

ADJECTIVE _____

NOUN _____

NOUN _____

NOUN _____

PLURAL NOUN _____

ADJECTIVE _____

PLURAL NOUN _____

NOUN _____

MAD LIBS®
MUSIC

"Music is the soul of the _____," said Pluto. "Music is
                                                   NOUN

music is music," said rap _____, I. B. Cool. These two
                                             NOUN

_____ philosophers were right on! When the beat is
      ADJECTIVE

right, who among us hasn't felt the _____ urge to snap
                                     ADJECTIVE

his/her _____ or stomp his/her _____
        BODY PART (PLURAL)   BODY PART (PLURAL)

or break out in a/an _____ _____? There's no
                     ADJECTIVE   NOUN

denying that music, whether it's a classical _____ by
                                     NOUN

Beethoven or a contemporary _____ by the Back
                          NOUN

Street _____, is a/an _____ influence
       PLURAL NOUN   ADJECTIVE

on our daily _____. Music does indeed soothe the
           PLURAL NOUN

savage _____.
       NOUN

From COOL MAD LIBS® • Copyright © 2001 by Price Stern Sloan,
a division of Penguin Putnam Books for Young Readers, New York.

MAD LIBS® is fun to play with friends, but you can also play it by yourself! To begin with, DO NOT look at the story on the page below. Fill in the blanks on this page with the words called for. Then, using the words you have selected, fill in the blank spaces in the story.

Now you've created your own hilarious MAD LIBS® game!

MOM'S MESSAGES

NUMBER _____

PLURAL NOUN _____

NOUN _____

ADJECTIVE _____

NOUN _____

VERB (PAST TENSE) _____

VERB _____

NOUN _____

BODY PART _____

NOUN _____

NOUN _____

NOUN _____

WEIRD SOUND _____

NOUN _____

ADJECTIVE _____

MAD LIBS®
MOM'S MESSAGES

Hi, it's your mother. Where are you? I've left over _____
                                                        NUMBER

_____ on your answering _____. Maybe you
   PLURAL NOUN   NOUN

forgot to turn the _____ ringer on. You're coming for
                          ADJECTIVE

_____ tonight, aren't you? Your certainly could use a/an
     NOUN

home-_____ meal. I'll call you later.... Hello, it's me
        VERB (PAST TENSE)

again. I'm at the doctor. Don't _____. I'm fine. I was in
                                        VERB

the market and I slipped on a/an _____ peel. The
                                            NOUN

doctor says I sprained my _____. I may have to wear
                                 BODY PART

a brace on the _____ or use crutches. But don't worry,
                     NOUN

honey. I'll call back.... Hello? Good, you're finally answering. What?

I can't speak any louder. I'm seeing a _____ at the
                                              NOUN

theater. Shakespeare's "Midsummer Night's _____."
                                                   NOUN

_____! I'm going to have to lower my _____; the
   WEIRD SOUND   NOUN

actors are giving me _____ looks. I'll call you back.
                            ADJECTIVE

From COOL MAD LIBS® • Copyright © 2001 by Price Stern Sloan,
a division of Penguin Putnam Books for Young Readers, New York.

MAD LIBS® is fun to play with friends, but you can also play it by yourself! To begin with, DO NOT look at the story on the page below. Fill in the blanks on this page with the words called for. Then, using the words you have selected, fill in the blank spaces in the story.

Now you've created your own hilarious MAD LIBS® game!

E-MAIL FROM AN INSOMNIAC

ADJECTIVE _____

PLURAL NOUN _____

NOUN _____

BODY PART _____

NOUN _____

ADJECTIVE _____

AN ANIMAL _____

ADJECTIVE _____

NOUN _____

VERB ENDING IN "ING" _____

NOUN _____

ADJECTIVE _____

NOUN _____

BODY PART (PLURAL) _____

VERB _____

ADJECTIVE _____

BODY PART _____

MAD LIBS®
E-MAIL FROM AN INSOMNIAC

Fellow insomniacs, I have some _____ news to share
ADJECTIVE

with you! Last night, for the first time in many _____,
PLURAL NOUN

I slept through the entire _____. The minute my _____
NOUN   BODY PART

hit the _____, I fell into a/an _____ sleep. Here
NOUN   ADJECTIVE

are some tips on how you can do it too:

1) Don't take _____ naps. They will keep you _____ at night.
AN ANIMAL   ADJECTIVE

2) Don't eat a heavy _____ before _____ to bed.
NOUN   VERB ENDING IN "ING"

3) Take a hot _____ or a/an _____ shower before
NOUN   ADJECTIVE

hitting the _____. It will relax all your _____.
NOUN   BODY PART (PLURAL)

4) And most importantly, make sure you _____ in a
VERB

comfortable bed that offers _____ support for your
ADJECTIVE

_____.
BODY PART

From COOL MAD LIBS® • Copyright © 2001 by Price Stern Sloan,
a division of Penguin Putnam Books for Young Readers, New York.

MAD LIBS® is fun to play with friends, but you can also play it by yourself! To begin with, DO NOT look at the story on the page below. Fill in the blanks on this page with the words called for. Then, using the words you have selected, fill in the blank spaces in the story.

Now you've created your own hilarious MAD LIBS® game!

THE APPOINTMENT

ADJECTIVE _____

NAME OF PERSON (FEMALE) _____

NOUN _____

SAME NAME OF PERSON (FEMALE) _____

NOUN _____

NOUN _____

ADVERB _____

VERB ENDING IN "ING" _____

NOUN _____

NUMBER _____

VERB _____

AN EVENT _____

NOUN _____

VERB (PAST TENSE) _____

NOUN _____

NAME OF PERSON (MALE) _____

PLURAL NOUN _____

MAD LIBS®
THE APPOINTMENT

(TO BE PERFORMED BY TWO _____ ACTORS)
                                        ADJECTIVE

Receptionist: Good Morning, _____'s Beauty
                              NAME OF PERSON (FEMALE)

and _____ Salon.
        NOUN

Woman on phone: I'd like to make an appointment with

_____ to have my _____ colored
SAME NAME OF PERSON (FEMALE)   NOUN

and _____ dried.
        NOUN

Receptionist: Oh, I'm _____ sorry. She isn't in today. She
                         ADVERB

had a _____ accident and broke her _____ in
      VERB ENDING IN "ING"   NOUN

_____ places.
  NUMBER

Woman on phone: Oh my, that's terrible, who can _____
                                                    VERB

me? I'm going to my daughter's _____ tonight. I can't
                                AN EVENT

possibly go without having my _____ styled and my eyebrows
                               NOUN

_____. And, I have just discovered a broken _____.
VERB (PAST TENSE)   NOUN

Receptionist: Relax madam. _____ is the answer
                            NAME OF PERSON (MALE)

to all your _____.
             PLURAL NOUN

From COOL MAD LIBS® • Copyright © 2001 by Price Stern Sloan,
a division of Penguin Putnam Books for Young Readers, New York.

MAD LIBS® is fun to play with friends, but you can also play it by yourself! To begin with, DO NOT look at the story on the page below. Fill in the blanks on this page with the words called for. Then, using the words you have selected, fill in the blank spaces in the story.

Now you've created your own hilarious MAD LIBS® game!

IT'S MAGIC

ANIMAL _____

OCCUPATION (PLURAL) _____

NOUN _____

NOUN _____

NOUN _____

VERB ENDING IN "ING" _____

BODY PART _____

PLURAL NOUN _____

ADJECTIVE _____

ANOTHER BODY PART _____

ANOTHER BODY PART _____

ADJECTIVE _____

ANIMAL _____

ADJECTIVE _____

ADVERB _____

MAD LIBS®
IT'S MAGIC

Ever since I was knee-high to a/an _____, I have loved
_{ANIMAL}

watching _____ perform their _____
_{OCCUPATION (PLURAL)}   _{NOUN}

tricks. If you've never seen a magician pull a/an _____
_{NOUN}

out of a/an _____ or catch a/an _____
_{NOUN}   _{VERB ENDING IN "ING"}

bullet in his _____, you've missed many of life's
_{BODY PART}

greatest _____. When I was seventeen, I gave _____
_{PLURAL NOUN}   _{ADJECTIVE}

thought to becoming a sleight-of- _____ expert.
_{ANOTHER BODY PART}

I was desperate to prove the _____ is quicker than
_{ANOTHER BODY PART}

the eye. Unfortunately, I didn't have the _____ skills to
_{ADJECTIVE}

do that. Today, I satisfy my craving for magic by going to Las Vegas

and watching Siegfried and Roy make a live _____
_{ANIMAL}

disappear into _____ air, and the casinos make my
_{ADJECTIVE}

money disappear just as _____.
_{ADVERB}

From COOL MAD LIBS® • Copyright © 2001 by Price Stern Sloan,
a division of Penguin Putnam Books for Young Readers, New York.

MAD LIBS® is fun to play with friends, but you can also play it by yourself! To begin with, DO NOT look at the story on the page below. Fill in the blanks on this page with the words called for. Then, using the words you have selected, fill in the blank spaces in the story.

Now you've created your own hilarious MAD LIBS® game!

JOHNNY COOL, P.I., CHAPTER ONE

FULL NAME OF PERSON (MALE) _____

NOUN _____

NOUN _____

NOUN _____

NOUN _____

NOUN _____

NOUN _____

BODY PART _____

NOUN _____

NOUN _____

ADJECTIVE _____

ADJECTIVE _____

NOUN _____

NOUN _____

ADVERB _____

MAD LIBS®
JOHNNY COOL, P.I.,
CHAPTER ONE

_____ , alias Johnny Cool, hated to make
FULL NAME OF PERSON (MALE)

decisions even when his _____ depended on it. He
NOUN

headed in the direction of an all-night _____ nestled
NOUN

between a self-service _____ station and a _____
NOUN   NOUN

parlor. He pushed open the diner _____ but didn't enter.
NOUN

The only street lamp on the dark _____ illuminated
NOUN

the fear on his _____. He was coming to another
BODY PART

decisive moment, and as always, it scared the _____ out
NOUN

of him. He took a deep _____ and entered the diner. It
NOUN

was almost _____. Johnny slumped into a/an _____
ADJECTIVE   ADJECTIVE

leather booth. He was **tired**. Every _____ in his body ached.
NOUN

His _____ was trembling. He needed coffee _____.
NOUN   ADVERB

From COOL MAD LIBS® • Copyright © 2001 by Price Stern Sloan,
a division of Penguin Putnam Books for Young Readers, New York.

MAD LIBS® is fun to play with friends, but you can also play it by yourself! To begin with, DO NOT look at the story on the page below. Fill in the blanks on this page with the words called for. Then, using the words you have selected, fill in the blank spaces in the story.

Now you've created your own hilarious MAD LIBS® game!

JOHNNY COOL, P.I., CHAPTER TWO

PLURAL NOUN _____

NOUN _____

COLOR _____

LIQUID _____

NOUN _____

VERB (PAST TENSE) _____

NOUN _____

NOUN _____

NOUN _____

BODY PART _____

ADJECTIVE _____

NOUN _____

PLURAL NOUN _____

NOUN _____

VERB ENDING IN "ING" _____

MAD LIBS®
JOHNNY COOL, P.I., CHAPTER TWO

Johnny Cool drummed his _____ on the _____ in
                        PLURAL NOUN   NOUN

the restaurant. The _____ -haired waitress brought him a
                         COLOR

cup of steaming, hot _____ and a grease-splattered
                            LIQUID

_____. He _____ at the menu. The moment he'd
     NOUN   VERB (PAST TENSE)

been dreading had come. Shivers ran up and down his _____.
                                                              NOUN

Beads of _____ poured over his _____ and
              NOUN   NOUN

down his _____. "Made up your mind?" asked the
              BODY PART

_____ waitress. Johnny reached for his voice, and in a
   ADJECTIVE

barely audible _____, said, "Ham and scrambled _____."
                    NOUN   PLURAL NOUN

"Okay" said the waitress, writing it down on her _____.
                                                        NOUN

"What kind of toast would you like—white or wheat?" Johnny Cool

could not handle another decision. He ran out of the diner

_____ at the top of his lungs.
VERB ENDING IN "ING"

From COOL MAD LIBS® • Copyright © 2001 by Price Stern Sloan,
a division of Penguin Putnam Books for Young Readers, New York.

MAD LIBS® is fun to play with friends, but you can also play it by yourself! To begin with, DO NOT look at the story on the page below. Fill in the blanks on this page with the words called for. Then, using the words you have selected, fill in the blank spaces in the story.

Now you've created your own hilarious MAD LIBS® game!

ICE-SKATING CHAMP

FULL NAME OF PERSON (FEMALE) _____

NOUN _____

ADJECTIVE _____

BODY PART (PLURAL) _____

ADJECTIVE _____

PLURAL NOUN _____

PLURAL NOUN _____

NOUN _____

NOUN _____

PLURAL NOUN _____

NOUN _____

LAST NAME OF PERSON IN ROOM _____

ADJECTIVE _____

ADJECTIVE _____

PERSON'S LAST NAME _____

NOUN _____

MAD LIBS®
ICE-SKATING CHAMP

Traditionally, _____ is as cool as the
FULL NAME OF PERSON (FEMALE)

_____ on which she skates. Last night, however, she
NOUN

surprised her _____ fans by pumping her _____
ADJECTIVE   BODY PART (PLURAL)

in the air and jumping into her _____ coach's
ADJECTIVE

_____ when her winning _____ were
PLURAL NOUN   PLURAL NOUN

flashed on the _____! Once again, America's five-time
NOUN

_____ champion had outdueled her four _____
NOUN   PLURAL NOUN

to win her third world _____. In a post-game interview,
NOUN

her coach, Pops _____, justified the
LAST NAME OF PERSON IN ROOM

champ's _____ enthusiasm: "Tonight she displayed
ADJECTIVE

_____ athleticism in performing the triple
ADJECTIVE

_____ loop and the double _____. I don't
PERSON'S LAST NAME   NOUN

think she's ever been better!"

From COOL MAD LIBS® • Copyright © 2001 by Price Stern Sloan,
a division of Penguin Putnam Books for Young Readers, New York.

MAD LIBS® is fun to play with friends, but you can also play it by yourself! To begin with, DO NOT look at the story on the page below. Fill in the blanks on this page with the words called for. Then, using the words you have selected, fill in the blank spaces in the story.

Now you've created your own hilarious MAD LIBS® game!

SNOWBOARDING INSTRUCTIONS

PERSON IN ROOM _____

OCCUPATION _____

VERB ENDING IN "ING" _____

PLURAL NOUN _____

ADJECTIVE _____

NOUN _____

ADJECTIVE _____

NOUN _____

ADVERB _____

BODY PART _____

PLURAL NOUN _____

NOUN _____

NOUN _____

ADVERB _____

ADJECTIVE _____

ADJECTIVE _____

NUMBER _____

NOUN _____

ADJECTIVE _____

MAD○LIBS®
SNOWBOARDING
INSTRUCTIONS

Good morning, everyone, I am ___creepy___, your
PERSON IN ROOM

snowboarding ___student___. How many of you have gone
OCCUPATION

___slacking___ before? Please raise your ___bolpes___.
VERB ENDING IN "ING"   PLURAL NOUN

None of you! Well, I feel I must warn you that while snowboarding is

___fully___ fun, it is also a dangerous ___bear___
ADJECTIVE   NOUN

and is much more difficult than skiing. This may come as a

___smooth___ surprise to you. But take a ___statel___ to
ADJECTIVE   NOUN

think about it. When you ski, your weight is ___quirkly___
ADVERB

distributed. You have one ___noes___ on each ski, helping
BODY PART

you maintain your balance. Snowboarding requires you to keep both

of your ___rocks___ on a narrow ___laptop___.
PLURAL NOUN   NOUN

Maintaining your ___love___ is ___non shonley___ hard.
NOUN   ADVERB

However, I promise if you are a/an ___short___ learner and
ADJECTIVE

pay ___blue___ attention, I will have you executing a
ADJECTIVE

___5___-degree ___lemonade___ grab within one
NUMBER   NOUN

___ugly___ week.
ADJECTIVE

From COOL MAD LIBS® • Copyright © 2001 by Price Stern Sloan,
a division of Penguin Putnam Books for Young Readers, New York.

MAD LIBS® is fun to play with friends, but you can also play it by yourself! To begin with, DO NOT look at the story on the page below. Fill in the blanks on this page with the words called for. Then, using the words you have selected, fill in the blank spaces in the story.

Now you've created your own hilarious MAD LIBS® game!

MOON FACTS

ADJECTIVE _____

NOUN _____

NOUN _____

ADJECTIVE _____

PLURAL NOUN _____

VERB ENDING IN "S" _____

NUMBER _____

NOUN _____

SAME NOUN _____

PERSON IN ROOM _____

ANOTHER PERSON IN ROOM _____

NOUN _____

PLURAL NOUN _____

BODY PART _____

PLURAL NOUN _____

ADJECTIVE _____

NOUN _____ _____

MAD☺LIBS®
MOON FACTS

1) Even though the moon first appears as a/an _____
ADJECTIVE

slice of light and finally becomes a full _____, it doesn't
NOUN

change its _____. The moon looks different as the _____
NOUN   ADJECTIVE

sun illuminates its different _____.
PLURAL NOUN

2) The moon _____ around the earth once in every
VERB ENDING IN "S"

_____ days.
NUMBER

3) If the moon were to be seen next to the earth it would look like a

tennis _____ next to a bowling _____.
NOUN   SAME NOUN

4) In 1969, _____ and _____,
PERSON IN ROOM   ANOTHER PERSON IN ROOM

from the Apollo _____, were the first human
NOUN

_____ to set _____ on the moon. Many
PLURAL NOUN   BODY PART

historians and _____ believe this to be the most
PLURAL NOUN

_____ achievement in the history of the _____.
ADJECTIVE   NOUN

From COOL MAD LIBS® • Copyright © 2001 by Price Stern Sloan,
a division of Penguin Putnam Books for Young Readers, New York.

MAD LIBS® is fun to play with friends, but you can also play it by yourself! To begin with, DO NOT look at the story on the page below. Fill in the blanks on this page with the words called for. Then, using the words you have selected, fill in the blank spaces in the story.

Now you've created your own hilarious MAD LIBS® game!

OFF THE EYE CHART

VERB ENDING IN "ING" _____

ADJECTIVE _____

NOUN _____

NOUN _____

SILLY WORD _____

PLURAL NOUN _____

NOUN _____

NOUN _____

PLURAL NOUN _____

PLURAL NOUN _____

NOUN _____

ADJECTIVE _____

PLURAL NOUN _____

ADVERB _____

MAD LIBS®
OFF THE EYE CHART

(DIALOGUE BETWEEN PATIENT AND EYE DOCTOR IN DOCTOR'S OFFICE)

Patient: Thanks for _____ me into your _____ .
                    VERB ENDING IN "ING"   ADJECTIVE

schedule. I have to go on tour in the morning.

Doctor: Are you a rock _____ ?
                       NOUN

Patient: Yes. I'm the lead _____ with the _____ band.
                           NOUN   SILLY WORD

Doctor: What kind of problems are you having with your _____ ?
                                                        PLURAL NOUN

Patient: When I try to read my _____ music, I have trouble
                                    NOUN

with the small _____ .
                       NOUN

Doctor: Have you ever worn eye _____ or
                                                PLURAL NOUN

contact _____ ?
                     PLURAL NOUN

Patient: Just _____ glasses.
                    NOUN

Doctor: Let's test your eyes. Look at the chart. When do the letters

become _____ ?
                   ADJECTIVE

Patient: What chart, Doc?

Doctor: The large one with _____ . Right in front of
                                        PLURAL NOUN

you . . . on the wall.

Patient: What wall?

Doctor: You _____ need glasses!
                   ADVERB

From COOL MAD LIBS® • Copyright © 2001 by Price Stern Sloan,
a division of Penguin Putnam Books for Young Readers, New York.

MAD LIBS® is fun to play with friends, but you can also play it by yourself! To begin with, DO NOT look at the story on the page below. Fill in the blanks on this page with the words called for. Then, using the words you have selected, fil! in the blank spaces in the story.

Now you've created your own hilarious MAD LIBS® game!

WORD GAMES

PLURAL NOUN _____

NOUN _____

NOUN _____

ADJECTIVE _____

PLURAL NOUN _____

PLURAL NOUN _____

NOUN _____

PLURAL NOUN _____

VERB _____

ADJECTIVE _____

ADJECTIVE _____

SAME ADJECTIVE _____

VERB _____

VERB ENDING IN "ING" _____

SAME ADJECTIVE _____

PLURAL NOUN _____

MAD LIBS®
WORD GAMES

In the early 1900s, crossword _____ only appeared in
                                    PLURAL NOUN

children's books. Today, _____ puzzles are in almost
                              NOUN

every _____ printed in the U.S. and throughout the
            NOUN

whole _____ world. More people do crossword
            ADJECTIVE

puzzles than smoke _____ or drink _____.
                        PLURAL NOUN   PLURAL NOUN

Some fanatics are known to do their puzzles even before they wash

their _____, brush their _____, or
            NOUN   PLURAL NOUN

_____ their breakfast. Another _____ word game
      VERB   ADJECTIVE

is _____ Libs. Not only is _____ Libs fun
      ADJECTIVE   SAME ADJECTIVE

to _____, but it is also an informative _____
      VERB   VERB ENDING IN "ING"

tool. By playing _____ Libs, kids learn how to use nouns,
                    SAME ADJECTIVE

adjectives, adverbs and _____.
                            PLURAL NOUN

From COOL MAD LIBS® • Copyright © 2001 by Price Stern Sloan,
a division of Penguin Putnam Books for Young Readers, New York.

MAD LIBS® is fun to play with friends, but you can also play it by yourself! To begin with, DO NOT look at the story on the page below. Fill in the blanks on this page with the words called for. Then, using the words you have selected, fill in the blank spaces in the story.

Now you've created your own hilarious MAD LIBS® game!

SNOWED IN

NOUN _____

ADVERB _____

PLURAL NOUN _____

NOUN _____

PLURAL NOUN _____

NOUN _____

PLURAL NOUN _____

NOUN _____

ADJECTIVE _____

PLURAL NOUN _____

PLURAL NOUN _____

ADJECTIVE _____

PLURAL NOUN _____

ADJECTIVE _____

NOUN _____

NOUN _____

MAD LIBS®
SNOWED IN

If you can't get out of your house because of a sudden
_____mountain_____ storm, don't panic. You'll be _____slowly_____
　　　NOUN　　　　　　　　　　　　　　　　　ADVERB

safe if you have the following _____pans_____ on hand:
　　　　　　　　　　　　　　　　PLURAL NOUN

1) At least one flash _____apple_____ in working condition with
　　　　　　　　　　　NOUN

plenty of extra _____cats_____.
　　　　　　PLURAL NOUN

2) A/an _____-operated radio that receives both AM and
　　　　　　　NOUN

C.B. _____.
　　　PLURAL NOUN

3) A first-aid _____.
　　　　　　　NOUN

4) A week's supply of _____ water.
　　　　　　　　　　　ADJECTIVE

5) Warm clothes. Preferably woolen _____, thermal
　　　　　　　　　　　　　　　　PLURAL NOUN

_____, and, of course, _____ underwear.
　PLURAL NOUN　　　　　　　　　　ADJECTIVE

6) Emergency numbers for the police and fire _____,
　　　　　　　　　　　　　　　　　　　　　PLURAL NOUN

your _____ doctor and a close _____ member
　　　ADJECTIVE　　　　　　　　　　　　NOUN

posted in a convenient _____.
　　　　　　　　　　　NOUN

From COOL MAD LIBS® • Copyright © 2001 by Price Stern Sloan,
a division of Penguin Putnam Books for Young Readers, New York.

MAD LIBS® is fun to play with friends, but you can also play it by yourself! To begin with, DO NOT look at the story on the page below. Fill in the blanks on this page with the words called for. Then, using the words you have selected, fill in the blank spaces in the story.

Now you've created your own hilarious MAD LIBS® game!

PENGUIN FACTS

PLURAL NOUN _____

LAST NAME OF PERSON IN ROOM _____

NOUN _____

PLURAL NOUN _____

ADVERB _____

VERB _____

ADJECTIVE _____

BODY PART (PLURAL) _____

PLURAL NOUN _____

VERB _____

NOUN _____

NOUN _____

BODY PART (PLURAL) _____

ADJECTIVE _____

PLURAL NOUN _____

PLURAL NOUN _____

MAD LIBS®
PENGUIN FACTS

Fellow bird _____, we are honored to have as our
PLURAL NOUN

speaker today Dr. _____ , America's
LAST NAME OF PERSON IN ROOM

foremost _____ on penguins and other cold-climate
NOUN

_____. The doctor has _____ agreed to answer
PLURAL NOUN   ADVERB

three questions before we _____ for lunch.
VERB

Doctor: First question, please.

Question: Why do penguins walk in such a/an _____ way?
ADJECTIVE

Doctor: You'd walk funny too if every step you took put your

_____ on frozen _____. Next!
BODY PART (PLURAL)   PLURAL NOUN

Question: How do penguins manage to _____ in such a
VERB

cold _____?
NOUN

Doctor: They have an abundance of _____ under their
NOUN

_____. This fat insulates them against _____
BODY PART (PLURAL)   ADJECTIVE

weather. Next!

Question: Why do we only see black and white penguins?

Doctor: Because they're very formal _____. They dress for
PLURAL NOUN

all occasions, especially sit-down _____.
PLURAL NOUN

From COOL MAD LIBS® • Copyright © 2001 by Price Stern Sloan,
a division of Penguin Putnam Books for Young Readers, New York.

MAD LIBS® is fun to play with friends, but you can also play it by yourself! To begin with, DO NOT look at the story on the page below. Fill in the blanks on this page with the words called for. Then, using the words you have selected, fill in the blank spaces in the story.

Now you've created your own hilarious MAD LIBS® game!

CLOSE DANCING IS COOL ... AGAIN

VERB ENDING IN "ING" _____

PLURAL NOUN _____

ADJECTIVE _____

PLURAL NOUN _____

SAME PLURAL NOUN _____

SAME PLURAL NOUN _____

PLURAL NOUN _____

NOUN _____

NOUN _____

PLURAL NOUN _____

NOUN _____

BODY PART _____

ADVERB _____

NUMBER _____

PLURAL NOUN _____

BODY PART _____

ADJECTIVE _____

MAD LIBS®
CLOSE DANCING IS COOL...
AGAIN

The waltz, the merengue, swing, and ballroom _____ are
                                            VERB ENDING IN "ING"

making a comeback with kids of all _____. A recent
                                    PLURAL NOUN

study shows a/an _____ percentage of students in
                  ADJECTIVE

elementary _____, middle _____, and even
            PLURAL NOUN   SAME PLURAL NOUN

high _____ are dropping their Phys Ed _____
      SAME PLURAL NOUN   PLURAL NOUN

in golf, bowling, and _____-pong to take up _____
                       NOUN   NOUN

dancing. Close dancing, in which partners hold each other's

_____ and put their _____ around each other's
 PLURAL NOUN   NOUN

_____ , is considered _____ cool these days.
 BODY PART   ADVERB

Sociologists predict that within the next _____ years, almost
                                           NUMBER

all teen _____ will once again be dancing cheek to
          PLURAL NOUN

_____ to the sound of a/an _____ band.
 BODY PART   ADJECTIVE

From COOL MAD LIBS® • Copyright © 2001 by Price Stern Sloan,
a division of Penguin Putnam Books for Young Readers, New York.

MAD LIBS® is fun to play with friends, but you can also play it by yourself! To begin with, DO NOT look at the story on the page below. Fill in the blanks on this page with the words called for. Then, using the words you have selected, fill in the blank spaces in the story.

Now you've created your own hilarious MAD LIBS® game!

TELEVISION PITCH FOR A BOOK ON HOW TO OVERCOME SHYNESS

NOUN _____

BODY PART _____

PLURAL NOUN _____

NOUN _____

NOUN _____

NOUN _____

ADVERB _____

ADVERB _____

NUMBER _____

NOUN _____

NOUN _____

PLURAL NOUN _____

VERB _____

ADVERB _____

NOUN _____

OCCUPATION (PLURAL) _____

MAD LIBS®
TELEVISION PITCH FOR A BOOK
ON HOW TO OVERCOME SHYNESS

(TO BE READ WITH GREAT SINCERITY)

Are you unable to introduce yourself to a member of the opposite

_____ without becoming red in the _____? Are
 NOUN   BODY PART

you uncomfortable in the presence of _____? Are you
                                        PLURAL NOUN

too shy to raise your _____ in class when you have to go to
                          NOUN

the _____? If you answered "no" to all of the above, you are
       NOUN

one cool _____. However, if you answered "yes" to any one
            NOUN

of the questions, you are _____ shy and _____ in
                             ADVERB   ADVERB

need of the nation's number _____ best-selling book,
                                 NUMBER

"Shyness is a State of _____."
                          NOUN

You can order this remarkable book by writing to the address now

showing on your TV _____. Send no _____.
                       NOUN   PLURAL NOUN

We'll _____ you later. If you can't wait to say "bye to shy,"
         VERB

call our toll-free number and we will rush the book to you

_____ at no extra _____. Call now, _____
 ADVERB   NOUN   OCCUPATION (PLURAL)

are standing by.

From COOL MAD LIBS® • Copyright © 2001 by Price Stern Sloan,
a division of Penguin Putnam Books for Young Readers, New York.

MAD LIBS® is fun to play with friends, but you can also play it by yourself! To begin with, DO NOT look at the story on the page below. Fill in the blanks on this page with the words called for. Then, using the words you have selected, fill in the blank spaces in the story.

Now you've created your own hilarious MAD LIBS® game!

IGLOO FACTS

NOUN _____

NOUN _____

NOUN _____

PLURAL NOUN _____

PLURAL NOUN _____

NOUN _____

ADJECTIVE _____

BODY PART _____

BODY PART _____

ADVERB _____

ADJECTIVE _____

PLURAL NOUN _____

NOUN _____

VERB _____

VERB _____

NOUN _____

MAD LIBS®
IGLOO FACTS

An igloo is an Eskimo ___stretsing___ or hut, which is made from
NOUN

blocks of hard-packed ___railroad___. A well-built ___king candycal___
NOUN   NOUN

not only provides comfort and warmth, but is also capable of

withstanding freezing ___tiels___ and howling ___pigs___.
PLURAL NOUN   PLURAL NOUN

In bygone years, if Eskimos traveling across a frozen ___Book___
NOUN

ran into a/an ___stinky___ snowstorm, one in which they couldn't
ADJECTIVE

see their ___toe___ in front of their ___lips___, they would
BODY PART   BODY PART

come to an abrupt stop and ___slcing___ construct an igloo. It
ADVERB

took them almost a/an ___dirty___ day to build one. Today, with
ADJECTIVE

modern ___grass___, an igloo can be completed in less than
PLURAL NOUN

a/an ___windmill___. And if you have enough food to eat, water to
NOUN

___trocking___ and candles to ___spelcting___, you can stay put
VERB   VERB

and safe for the rest of your ___dog___.
NOUN

From COOL MAD LIBS® • Copyright © 2001 by Price Stern Sloan,
a division of Penguin Putnam Books for Young Readers, New York.

MAD LIBS® is fun to play with friends, but you can also play it by yourself! To begin with, DO NOT look at the story on the page below. Fill in the blanks on this page with the words called for. Then, using the words you have selected, fill in the blank spaces in the story.

Now you've created your own hilarious MAD LIBS® game!

A RECIPE FOR ICE CUBES

ADJECTIVE _____

NOUN _____

NOUN _____

VERB _____

A LIQUID _____

ANOTHER LIQUID _____

ANOTHER LIQUID _____

COLOR _____

VERB _____

VERB _____

NUMBER _____

ADJECTIVE _____

ADVERB _____

BODY PART (PLURAL) _____

VERB _____

VERB _____

To make _____ ice cubes, first find a tray with molds
　　　　　　ADJECTIVE

shaped like a _____ or a _____. Then _____
　　　　　　　　NOUN　　　　　　　　NOUN　　　　　　　　VERB

once while holding the tray. Fill the molds with _____,
　　　　　　　　　　　　　　　　　　　　　　　　　A LIQUID

or even _____, but for the best results always use
　　　　　ANOTHER LIQUID

_____ . It can even be dyed _____ if you wish.
ANOTHER LIQUID　　　　　　　　　　　　　　COLOR

_____ carefully when placing the tray in the freezer. Allow
　　VERB

the cubes to _____ for at least _____ minutes until
　　　　　　　VERB　　　　　　　　　　NUMBER

they are completely _____ . Remove the tray _____,
　　　　　　　　　ADJECTIVE　　　　　　　　　　　ADVERB

and jiggle with your _____ until the cubes _____.
　　　　　　　　　BODY PART (PLURAL)　　　　　　　　　　VERB

Add to your favorite drink and _____!
　　　　　　　　　　　　　　VERB

From COOL MAD LIBS® • Copyright © 2001 by Price Stern Sloan,
a division of Penguin Putnam Books for Young Readers, New York.

This book is published by

PSS!
PRICE STERN SLOAN

whose other splendid titles include
such literary classics as

Ad Lib Mad Libs®

Best of Mad Libs®

Camp Daze Mad Libs®

Christmas Carol Mad Libs®

Christmas Fun Mad Libs®

Cool Mad Libs®

Dance Mania Mad Libs®

Dear Valentine Letters Mad Libs®

Dinosaur Mad Libs®

Diva Girl Mad Libs®

Dude, Where's My Mad Libs®

Family Tree Mad Libs®

Fun in the Sun Mad Libs®

Girls Just Wanna Have Mad Libs®

Goofy Mad Libs®

Grab Bag Mad Libs®

Graduation Mad Libs®

Grand Slam Mad Libs®

Happily Ever Mad Libs®

Happy Birthday Mad Libs®

Haunted Mad Libs®

Holly, Jolly Mad Libs®

Kid Libs Mad Libs®

Letters From Camp Mad Libs®

Letters to Mom & Dad Mad Libs®

Mad About Animals Mad Libs®

Mad Libs® for President

Mad Libs® from Outer Space

Mad Libs® in Love

Mad Libs® on the Road

Mad Mad Mad Mad Mad Libs®

Monster Mad Libs®

More Best of Mad Libs®

Night of the Living Mad Libs®

Ninjas Mad Libs®

Off-the-Wall Mad Libs®

The Original #1 Mad Libs®

P. S. I Love Mad Libs®

Peace, Love, and Mad Libs®

Pirates Mad Libs®

Prime-Time Mad Libs®

Rock 'n' Roll Mad Libs®

Slam Dunk Mad Libs®

Sleepover Party Mad Libs®

Son of Mad Libs®

Sooper Dooper Mad Libs®

Spooky Mad Libs®

Straight "A" Mad Libs®

Totally Pink Mad Libs®

Undead Mad Libs®

Upside Down Mad Libs®

Vacation Fun Mad Libs®

We Wish You a Merry Mad Libs®

Winter Games Mad Libs®

You've Got Mad Libs®

and many, many more!
Mad Libs® are available wherever books are sold.